Also by Tracey A. Breen
Burdens As Blessings – 2015
In The Weeds – 2018

The Low Oxalate Cookbook

50 Easy Low Oxalate Recipes

Tracey A. Breen

Contact author at: www.thelowoxalatecookbook.com

ISBN: 978-0692088210

Limit of Liability and Disclaimer of Warranty:

The recipes and information in this book are provided for educational and informational purposes only and is provided "as is." No representation or warranties with respect to the accuracy or completeness of the contents of the cookbook are made and I specifically disclaim any implied warranties of merchantability or fitness for any particular purpose.

The definition for low oxalate is defined by the Harvard list as interpreted by this author.

All readers should consult with their physicians before making any changes to their current diet or menu plans. This book is not intended as a substitute for the medical advice of physicians. The reader should regularly consult a physician in matters relating to his/her health with respect to any symptoms that may require a diagnosis or medical attention.

I do not claim to be a doctor, nutritionist or dietitian. The information in The Low Oxalate Cookbook is my personal opinion and does not replace professional, medical or nutritional advice.

10 9 8 7 6 5 4 3 2 1

First Edition

To the first cooks in my life ~
My Mom Georgialee and my Grandma B's

Contents

SIDE DISHES 28

APPETIZERS/SNACKS 35

DESSERTS 48

Introduction

Welcome

Welcome to *The Low Oxalate Cookbook*! Enjoy 50 recipes for real people which happen to be low oxalate. Easy and simple recipes any person can make, bake or cook. The ingredients are easily accessible, cost conscious and low oxalate. An occasional moderate oxalate ingredient is included, but the serving size will limit the oxalate value.

My Journey

I am not affiliated with the University Of Chicago. After my tangle with a kidney stone I investigated and researched the how, why and how can I avoid future kidney stones. I found myself in the group of many who are unsatisfied with the answers from an urologist. I left the urologist office with the standard drink more water and eat less salt advice; and that may very well be absolutely true for some kidney stone makers.

My research led me to the University Of Chicago Kidney site which has a wealth of knowledge and is a labor of love for Dr. Fredric Coe and Jill Harris. I am not aware of any other website which is more comprehensive to cover all aspects of kidney stones and concentrates on prevention. The authenticity of Dr. Coe and Jill Harris is evident throughout the site to help a patient understand what to do and how to do it.

The information is valuable to all patients making a lifestyle change due to kidney stones irrespective if oxalates are or are not an issue in your menu. The first nugget of advice you will find in the site is: do you need a low oxalate diet? If your test values do not indicate the need then a low oxalate menu is not necessary.

Balancing Nutrition and Oxalates

As I googled my way through the good, bad and sometimes wacky information on the internet by chance I clicked back to the University Of Chicago site to check a fact. I happened upon an announcement by Jill Harris that she was starting an online class using her years of kidney stone prevention experience to help people prevent kidney stones, understand a balanced diet and offer support. I took a chance and signed up for the first course offered by Jill Harris, and the course under promised and over delivered to the delight of the first group of participants and those who continue to take the class. Information on the class by Jill Harris on her website at https://jillharriscoaching.com/ .

Jill's class is a comprehensive deep dive into the connection between sodium, calcium, dairy, sugar and oxalates in forming kidney stones. Support, suggestions and solid nutritional advice is given in a small group setting that also personalizes a balanced diet to your unique medical conditions. Every person has their own medical conditions, food preference or food restrictions which makes incorporating a low oxalate menu even more challenging.

From A Kidney Stone to a Cookbook

On my lifestyle site The Savvy Age I share my family recipes and thought why not incorporate and tweak recipes to be a low oxalate recipe. One of the first problems when discovering that a low oxalate menu is in your future is finding ready-to-cook recipes. The lists and information are overwhelming and there is a learning curve to incorporate low oxalate food into your and/or your families' menu. Plus any food restrictions. Plus food preferences. And on and on…

So as I traveled the path of low oxalates I began tweaking family recipes and creating new low oxalate recipes along the way. From a kidney stone to the University of Chicago Kidney site to Jill Harris's class to the Admin of the Low Ox Foodies Facebook group and now to a cookbook.

How to Define Low Oxalate

Low oxalate values for this cookbook are measured by Harvard T. H. Chan School of Public Health known in this book as "The Harvard List." Simple right! It can be that simple. This is the most extensive list by an authoritative source. The web address for the Harvard list is in the Resources section at the back of the book. The list has been updated and is also available on the University Of Chicago kidney site.

Lists, Lists and More Lists

There is no shortage of oxalate lists. Many are well sourced and many are not. I came upon the University Of Chicago Kidney website literally in the emergency room googling from the bed and somewhere between gripping the bed rails and waiting to find out the fate of my new foe EO (Evil One, haven't we all named a kidney stone or few?)

While googling between pain bursts and after the nurse asked me if there was anything she could do? To which my response was, "Feel free to wheel me out to the street and let an 18 wheeler run over the bed if it will help the pain…" I also found the Harvard list. Thankfully EO was on the move and traveling toward its final destination, and then the research began in earnest.

Also on the How to Eat a Low Oxalate Diet page is an interesting paper in which the authors compared the oxalate value of foods from different sources. *The Oxalate Content of Foods: A Tangled Web* from 2014 succinctly explains the problems with measuring oxalates and the different lists. A definite addition to your resource library particularly if you are new to a low oxalate menu.

A Word on Sodium

Sodium is used very sparingly in these recipes. Chances are if you have found this cookbook you have already lowered your sodium intake; sodium is to be added after the recipe in most recipes.

A Word on Spices

Low oxalate herbs are frequently used in the recipes, but spices with a kick are not. Many who follow a low oxalate menu have additional medical conditions which may or may not restrict spices. If you know a spice is low oxalate then absolutely kick up the recipe a notch! Low oxalate cooks are inherently creative and you know which spices you or your family favor.

A Word on Desserts

Yes, Virginia there is sugar in some of these desserts. The desserts are ready to serve to your family or guests with a bonus of low oxalate ingredients. This also means one serving for low oxalate watchers.

A Word on Vegetarian and Diabetic Requirements

I am keeping it real. If you are seeking low oxalate recipes for a vegetarian or diabetic menu many of these recipes are more than likely not be appropriate for your menu. Some recipes will qualify, but most will not satisfy the special dietary needs.

BREAKFAST

Mini Ham Cheese And Egg Cups

Makes 8 cups

Ingredients

- 6 eggs
- 4 egg whites
- 2 tablespoons milk (can use fat free)
- 3 tablespoons minced chives
- ¾ cup diced ham
- 1 cup shredded cheddar cheese (can use low sodium, low fat cheese)
- Cooking spray
- Salt and white pepper to taste

Directions

1. Prepare a mini muffin pan by greasing the inside of each cup and the top of the pan.
2. Preheat oven to 375 degrees F.
3. In a medium size bowl combine the egg, egg whites and milk. Whisk.
4. Evenly divide the ham and cheese into each muffin cup.
5. Pour the egg mixture over the ham and cheese into each muffin cup. Fill to three quarters of the muffin cup.
6. Bake 20–25 minutes.
7. Use a toothpick or knife inserted in the middle to check if the egg cup is done. The toothpick/knife should come out clean.
8. Remove.
9. Gently take a knife and run the knife around the edge to ensure the cups come out of the muffin pan cleanly.

Tips & Notes:

These cups can also be made with all cheese. I usually make half ham and cheese cups and half just cheese cups. Light, airy and yummy! Make ahead and freeze for the future.

Cauliflower Hashbrowns

Serves 4

Ingredients

- → 1 bag frozen cauliflower rice thawed (about 3 cups)
- → 1 large egg
- → ½ cup diced onion
- → 3 tablespoons corn starch
- → Virgin olive oil
- → Optional 1 cup shredded cheese
- → Salt and white pepper to taste
- → Mix all ingredients.

Directions

1. Heat a large skillet over medium high heat.
2. Add 1 tablespoon olive oil and heat.
3. Add large spoonfuls of the cauliflower and use a spatula to shape into a patty.
4. Cook until top is brown about five minutes.
5. Flip and cook an additional five minutes.
6. Plate and serve.

Tips & Notes:

This is my favorite cauliflower recipe. I use frozen riced cauliflower to speed up the prep time. If you are using fresh cauliflower grate enough for 3 cups. Cheese is optional. Add garlic for a more robust flavor if desired.

Banana Pancakes
Serves 1–2

Ingredients

- 1 medium banana
- 2 eggs
- Splash of vanilla
- Splash of baking powder
- Cooking spray or oil

Directions

1. Mash the banana, add eggs, vanilla and baking powder.
2. Prepare a medium size skillet with cooking spray or oil so pancakes do not stick.
3. Use 2 tablespoons of batter per pancake. The batter is slightly lumpy and a bit testy to flip.
4. Cook each pancake until the bottom is golden brown (peek!)
5. Slowly flip each pancake and cook until batter has set.
6. Serve.

Tips & Notes:

Add instant oatmeal to make a firmer pancake. Add blueberries for a fun twist. I add a splash of baking powder to make the pancake fluffier. No doubt these pancakes taste like bananas so if you don't like bananas …

Coconut Flour Bread

Makes one loaf

Ingredients

→ 6 eggs at room temperature
→ ½ cup coconut oil (melt and cool)
→ 1 tablespoon honey
→ ¾ cup coconut flour (I like Bob's Red Mill)
→ ½ teaspoon sea salt
→ 1 teaspoon baking powder

Directions

1. Preheat oven to 350 degree F.
2. Grease a bread pan with coconut oil or cooking spray.
3. In a large mixing bowl combine the coconut oil, honey and eggs and mix.
4. Add coconut flour, salt and baking powder.
5. Mix until smooth.
6. Let batter sit for five minutes.
7. Pour batter into the pan.
8. Bake approximately 35 to 40 minutes until top is golden brown and the middle is clean when a toothpick is inserted.

Tips & Notes:

This is the best coconut flour bread recipe I have tried yet! Love to use this as a toasting bread. Just a hint of coconut flavor in this dense bread.

Oxalate Friendly Granola
Serves 4–6

All low oxalate. Sprinkle on yogurt or take with you to work for a very natural snack.

Ingredients

→ 1 cups rolled oats
→ 1 cup oat bran
→ ¼ cup flax seeds
→ ¼ cup sunflower seeds
→ ½ cup dried and unsweetened fruit (apples, apricots or cranberries)
→ 2–3 tablespoons honey or maple syrup
→ 2 tablespoons melted coconut oil
→ ½ teaspoon vanilla extract
→ Dash of sea salt

Directions

1. Preheat oven to 300 degrees F.
2. Line a baking sheet with parchment paper.
3. In a large bowl mix all ingredients. This will be sticky! Feel free to use your hands or disposable cooking gloves.
4. Spread the mixture on the baking sheet in a thin layer.
5. Bake 10 minutes until just lightly toasted.
6. Cool.
7. Store in an airtight container for up to two weeks.

Tips & Notes:

This is a mix and match recipe and very flexible—but beware of dried fruits. The water is removed so an unassuming fruit can become higher in oxalate when dried. Choose wisely. Switch around the ingredients to your liking and experiment.

Baked Eggs
Serves 6

Ingredients

- 6 eggs
- Cooking spray of your choice
- Salt and white pepper to taste
- Optional low oxalate veggies or ham or bacon or all!

Directions

1. Standard size muffin pan.
2. Spray each muffin cup with cooking spray.
3. Preheat oven to 350 degrees F.
4. Crack one egg per muffin cup.
5. Sprinkle with salt and pepper to taste.
6. Cook for 12–15 minutes until the egg is set.

   Optional: add vegetables, cheese, ham or bacon. Add to the bottom of the muffin cup before egg is cracked into cup.

Tips & Notes:

My first reaction when I started trying this method of making eggs was where have I been! What an easy way to make eggs for the week. These eggs are perfect alone or use for an egg sandwich or healthy add on to salad. Simply remove from the refrigerator and reheat!

LUNCH/
DINNER

Flaxseed Meatloaf

Serves 4

Ingredients

- 1 lbs Ground Round
- ⅛ cup flaxseed meal
- ¼ teaspoon salt
- 1 egg beaten
- ⅛ cup chopped onion
- 1 ½ cloves garlic
- Ketchup optional /to taste

Directions

1. Preheat oven to 375 degrees Fahrenheit.
2. Grease a casserole dish or parchment lined baking sheet.
3. In a medium sized bowl combine all ingredients.
4. Remove the ingredients and shape into a meatloaf.
5. Place the meatloaf in the casserole dish or on a baking sheet.
6. If desired use a meatloaf pan.
7. Bake 45–55 minutes.
8. Remove and top or serve with ketchup if desired.

Tips & Notes:

This is a great recipe to incorporate flaxseed meal and you will hardly notice the flaxseed is in the meatloaf. Expect a slight nutty flavor. It can easily be doubled or made into mini meatloaves.

This is a recipe which can be tweaked to how you usually make meatloaf. If you like ketchup in the meatloaf then use it. If you like ketchup on the top of the meatloaf or on the side that works too! Or leave out the ketchup.

Cauliflower Macaroni and Cheese

Serves 4

Ingredients

→ 1 head of cauliflower, break into small florets
→ ½ cup half and half
→ 1 tablespoons butter
→ 1 cup shredded cheddar cheese, use your favorite
→ White pepper to taste
→ Herbs of your choice to taste

Directions

1. Prepare 8" by 8" baking dish with cooking spray.
2. Cook the cauliflower either by roasting, steaming or boiling.
3. Heat the half and half, butter and cheddar cheese over medium heat until smooth.
4. Toss together the cooked cauliflower florets and cheese sauce.
5. Serve immediately.

Tips & Notes:

This is another quick and easy dish to use cauliflower. Replace the half and half with heavy cream for a creamier sauce; to lower calories use milk and the sauce will be less creamy.

Mince and Tatties–The Low Oxalate Way

Serves 4

Ingredients

- → 1 pound of minced beef (ground round, ground sirloin, ground steak)
- → 1 small diced onion
- → ½ tablespoon of flour
- → 1 cup of beef stock (use low sodium if desired)
- → Mashed cauliflower.
- → Butter and milk as desired for mashed cauliflower.
- → Salt and pepper to taste
- → Optional: Peas, dash of Worcester sauce for a kick.

I know you know how to make mashed cauliflower. Mashed cauliflower is the go-to substitute for mashed potatoes if eating a low oxalate menu. You will be making the mashed cauliflower in conjunction with cooking the beef.

Directions

Begin by making the mashed cauliflower first so the mashed cauliflower will be finished in time to be finished with the mince.

1. In medium heat in a large skillet, brown the beef and onions.
2. Once cooked, add flour to mixture. If desired add peas.
3. Pour beef stock over mixture, lower heat and simmer 15–20 minutes.
4. Serve the mashed cauliflower with the mince. Your choice: Mix both together or eat separately on the same plate.

Tips & Notes:

Mince and Tatties is a traditional Scottish recipe. This is a tastes great, but not the prettiest of meals I am warning you now. A stick to the bones meal reminiscent of Grandma's depression era meals. Mashed cauliflower Alert—check out my favorite kitchen hacks to ensure a smooth and creamy cauliflower mash is achieved!

Ham and Broccoli Crustless Quiche

Serves 6

Ingredients

- 1 cup diced low salt ham
- 1 cup broccoli florets (frozen or fresh)
- 4 beaten eggs
- 4 egg whites
- 1/4 cup water
- 1 cup low fat cottage cheese

Directions

1. Prepare a 9" pie, baking dish or quiche dish with cooking spray.
2. Heat oven to 375 degrees F.
3. Prepare your broccoli by pre cooking either in the microwave or on the stove top.
4. Dice the ham while the broccoli is cooking.
5. Using a large bowl, whisk the eggs, egg whites and water.
6. Now add the cottage cheese and whisk briskly The cottage cheese should become fairly smooth and mix in with the egg mixture.
7. Pour into prepared dish.
8. Place the broccoli and ham into the mixture.
9. Bake for 30 to 35 minutes. Check at the 30 minute mark.
10. Check that the quiche has set by inserting a knife or toothpick in the middle – it should come out clean. As this quiche has no crust, then the top will become slightly golden brown.

Tips & Notes:

This is a very flexible recipe and if desired the ham can be omitted and fill the quiche with your favorite low oxalate veggies. Serve for brunch, lunch or dinner with a salad.

Grandma's Favorite Mac N Cheese Recipe

Serves 4

Ingredients

- → 8 ounces of elbow macaroni (can use gluten free)
- → 8 ounces block cheese of your choice. I use sharp cheddar. (can use low sodium cheese)
- → 2 tablespoons butter or margarine
- → 1 cup milk of your choice
- → Crushed Ritz crackers or breadcrumbs (plain or gluten free)

Directions

1. Boil the macaroni to your desired firmness.
2. While boiling macaroni cut the block cheese into ½ inch cubes.
3. Cut the butter into dab size pieces.
4. Drain macaroni.
5. Grease a 2 QT glass baking dish.
6. Begin layering dish.

Order of Layers

1. Layer of macaroni on bottom of dish.
2. Add the cheese squares and butter dots on top of the macaroni. Approximately 3/4 of the macaroni should be covered.
3. Repeat two more times.
4. Pour milk into baking dish, but not the entire cup at once.
5. The milk should cover 3/4 of the mixture. Add the milk and look at the baking dish from the side to decide when to stop.
6. Cook for 30–35 minutes at 350 degrees F.

Tips & Notes:

Layering is the key to this dish for even cheese throughout. This is our old-fashioned version of the family Mac n Cheese recipe. Old School. Old Fashioned. No Roux. Grandma did not use a roux! The ingredients in this version are so flexible; use low fat, low sodium, fat free cheeses or milk. The richer the ingredients the richer the dish. Let your guests add the salt and pepper to taste. Even add cooked ham or broccoli in to make a robust meal.

Salmon Balls

Serves 4

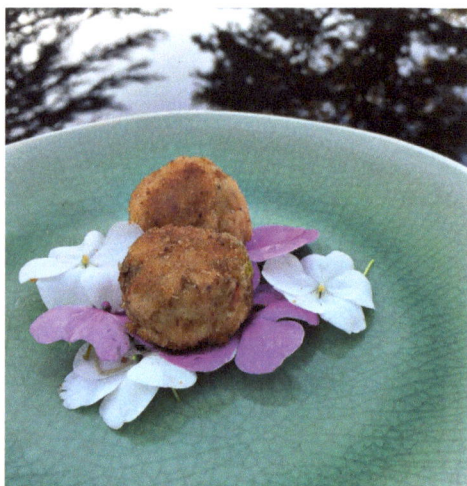

Ingredients

- 1 can of canned salmon (14.75 oz.)
- 1 beaten egg
- 2 tablespoons of onion
- ½ cup of bread crumbs (use a lower oxalate bread)
- Olive oil to fry

Directions

1. Combine all ingredients except the bread crumbs.
2. Form into bite size balls.
3. Roll each ball into the breadcrumbs.
4. Lightly coat the skillet with oil. You do not need alot of oil.
5. Heat the skillet and oil to medium high heat.
6. Gently add the salmon balls to the heat. You are warming the salmon balls and also forming a nice crunchy crust. This is not deep frying a salmon ball!
7. With your tongs, gently—oh so gently—rotate the sides of each salmon ball to form an even crust. This step takes the most time, but you will use much much less oil than actually deep frying a salmon ball.
8. Remove from heat and serve promptly.

Tips & Notes:

Who said salmon ball! I love making fish balls to serve with a low oxalate salad; they add a little crunch and the healthy Omegas to your meal. Catfish, Tilapia and whitefish all work well when making a fish ball.

Mock Lettuce Wraps

Serves 4

Ingredients

- 2 breasts of leftover seasoned chicken or rotisserie chicken diced
- 1 can of water chestnuts chopped
- ⅔ cup diced mushroom
- 1 teaspoon minced garlic
- 2 tablespoons chopped chives
- 1 head of Iceberg lettuce
- 1 tablespoon olive oil
- Stir Fry Sauce
- 2 tablespoons low sodium soy sauce
- 2 tablespoons of brown sugar
- ½ teaspoon rice vinegar

Directions

1. Chop the water chestnuts and chicken into dice size pieces.
2. Stir fry sauce: Mix together: low sodium soy sauce, brown sugar, and rice wine vinegar.
3. Heat one tablespoon of oil in a large skillet at medium high heat.
4. Add the diced chicken, mushrooms, garlic and water chestnuts to the pan and then add the sauce. Cook for five minutes on medium heat then lower heat for an additional three to five minutes.
5. Tear lettuce leaves off the head and make a cup.
6. Add the chicken and ready to serve!

Tips & Notes:

Use leaves of iceberg lettuce as a wrap or serve over white rice. The special sauce by the famous Chinese restaurant chain is not used due to the sugar content. Simply double the stir fry sauce to add more sauce especially if serving over rice.

Grandma's Hamburger Mash

Serves 4

Ingredients

- 1 pound ground beef
- 1 small cooking onion chopped
- 1 tablespoon minced garlic.
- 4 servings of corn 1 can drained
- 4 servings of peas 1 can drained

Directions

1. Spray a large skillet with cooking spray and use medium heat. Add the ground beef, garlic, onions and brown.
2. Remove from heat and drain fat.
3. Add peas and corn. Mix all ingredients.
4. Serve hot.

Tips & Notes:

This is another quick and stick to your bones recipe from Grandma. It is not a very pretty recipe (there I said it), but is very tasty especially if served over rice. Add mushrooms if desired or even just add all peas or all corn—anything goes. Salt and pepper to taste for the oxalate friendly.

City Chicken

Serves 4

Ingredients

- ½ pound boneless pork cut into 1" cubes
- ½ pound veal cut into 1" cubes
- 1 small chopped onion
- 2 eggs beaten
- ½ cup flour
- Pepper, garlic and onion salt or powder to taste
- 2–3 tablespoons oil
- ½ cup water plus as needed
- 4 inch wood skewers

Directions

1. Cut the pork and veal into 1" cubes. Alternate the cubes on 4" wood skewers.
2. Prepare a bowl with beaten eggs.
3. Prepare a bowl with the flour dredge. Add pepper, garlic and onion salt to taste into the flour. A healthy shake of each.
4. Assembly line style dunk each skewer in the eggs and then dredge in flour. Set aside.
5. Heat the oil in a large skillet to medium low heat. Brown each skewer of city chicken.
6. Add the chopped onions.
7. Add ½ cup water. Cover skillet and reduce heat to low approximately one hour. Check water and add water if needed so the water does not boil off.

Tips & Notes

The first question is usually, "where is the chicken?" There is no chicken in City Chicken! Veal can be difficult to find so substitute all pork. Here in the midwest I can still find the skewers pre made at the butcher occasionally. The water is the key for tender city chicken.

Baked Coconut Flour Shrimp

Serves 2–3

Ingredients

- 18–20 deveined shrimp with tail off (allow for jumpers)
- 1 egg white
- 2 tablespoons water
- ½ cup coconut flour (I like Bob's Red Mill)
- ⅛ cup coconut flakes, shredded and unsweetened
- ½ teaspoon garlic powder
- White pepper to taste

Directions

1. Preheat oven to 350 degrees F.
2. Line a baking pan with parchment paper.
3. Prepare the assembly line.
4. In a bowl whisk the coconut flour, coconut shreds, garlic powder. Whisking helps lighten the flour.
5. In a second bowl whisk the egg whites and water.
6. Take each shrimp and dip into the egg white mix then generously dredge in the flour.
7. Place coated shrimp on a baking sheet.
8. Bake for 13–15 minutes until golden brown and crispy.

Tips & Notes:

Careful not to overcook the shrimp as no one loves a tough shrimp! Serve with a salad and this makes a very very low oxalate meal.

Cucumber Soup

Serves 4

Ingredients

- 2 pounds large seedless cucumbers chopped (these are the 12 inch long cucumbers)
- 1 ½ cups greek yogurt
- 3 tablespoons lemon juice
- 1 shallot chopped
- 1 clove of garlic chopped
- ⅓ cup fresh dill
- ½ cup red onion chopped
- ¼ cup olive oil

Directions

1. In a blender or food processor add chopped cucumbers, yogurt, lemon juice, shallot, garlic, dill and olive oil.
2. Blend until smooth.
3. Refrigerate overnight.
4. Ladle individual portions and garnish with a drizzle of olive oil, red onion and a few diced cucumber bits.

Tips & Notes:

If you do not have access to the long seedless cucumbers substitute regular cucumbers, but the seeds must be removed. Two pounds plus of cucumbers are needed.

Turkey Reuben

Serves 2

Ingredients

- ½ pound low sodium turkey breast
- 4 slices swiss cheese
- Favorite coleslaw
- 2 slices of bread
- Butter

Directions

1. Preheat oven to 350 degrees F.
2. Line a baking sheet with parchment paper.
3. Place two slices of bread on lined baking sheet.
4. Butter each slice.
5. Place baking pan in oven for about five minutes to lightly toast the bread.
6. Remove from oven add 2 slices of cheese to each slice of bread.
7. Add 2–3 slices of turkey.
8. Return to oven to let the cheese melt and the turkey is warmed.
9. Once the cheese is melted remove from oven.
10. Plate and add a healthy serving of coleslaw to the top of each slice.

Tips & Notes:

This sandwich is served open face to lower the total oxalate value as most breads are moderate to high depending upon the flour used. If using a coconut flour or oat flour bread then make a sandwich!

SALADS

Blue Cheese Slaw

Serves 4

Ingredients

- → 1 bag favorite cabbage coleslaw mix
- → 1 cup crumbled blue cheese
- → ⅓ cup mayonnaise
- → 4 green onions

Directions

1. Mix all ingredients together and chill.

Tips & Notes:

Serve on top of ham or turkey as a tasty topper. No carrots in this coleslaw due to oxalate level of carrot. If you are a bacon fan add a few crumbles of low sodium bacon or turkey bacon.

Taco Salad

Serves 4

Ingredients

- 1 pound ground beef
- 1 medium diced onion
- 1–2 gloves garlic to taste
- Flaxseed chips, corn chips or tortilla chips
- Shredded iceberg or romaine lettuce
- 1 bag of shredded cheese or 2 cups, your favorite yellow or white
- Favorite low oxalate vegetables— cucumber, zucchini, yellow, squash, a few cherry tomatoes

Directions

1. Brown ground beef with onions and garlic.
2. Add a layer of shredded lettuce to a large serving plate.
3. Top lettuce with seasoned beef, vegetables and cheese.
4. Serve with chips family style.

Tips & Notes:

Taco Salad is always a quick and easy favorite. Flaxseed chips can easily be substituted for tortilla chips if desired. Use low sodium shredded cheese. Add olives on the side for oxalate friendly guests. Corn chips and flaxseed chips are low oxalate; tortilla chips are medium.

Maurice Salad

Serves 6

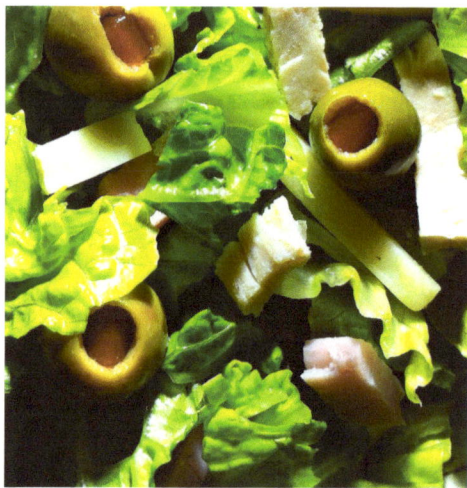

Ingredients

- → 1 pound turkey breast julienned
- → 1 pound ham julienned
- → 1 pound swiss cheese julienned
- → 1 hard boiled egg chopped
- → 1 head of lettuce chopped or shredded
- → ½ cup sweet gherkin pickles
- → 2 large pimento green olives (optional)

Dressing

- → 2 teaspoons white vinegar
- → 1 ½ teaspoons of lemon juice
- → 1 ½ teaspoons of sugar
- → 1 ½ teaspoons of dijon mustard
- → ¼ teaspoon of dry mustard
- → 1 cup mayonnaise
  Combine all ingredients with a whisk and make sure to dissolve the sugar.

Directions

1. Combine salad ingredients in a large bowl and fold.
2. Add the dressing.
3. Top each salad with 2 green olives.

Tips & Notes:

This version of the Maurice Salad is legendary in our area. It was and is still remembered as the signature dish of J.L. Hudson the iconic department store. Substitute low sodium versions of ham, turkey and swiss if desired. You will find this version deconstructed instead of all ingredients mixed together. I like to separate the ingredients to make it easier for a guest to avoid any undesired ingredients. Olives are high oxalate so best avoided unless you are an olive aficionado and wish to allocate your oxalates there. 10 olives = 18 mg oxalate, 2 olives = approximately 3.6 mg oxalate.

Cauliflower Faux Potato Salad

Serves 4

Ingredients

- One head of cauliflower or 1 bag frozen cauliflower cooked
- ⅔ cup mayonnaise
- 1 tablespoon apple cider vinegar
- 1 tablespoon Dijon mustard
- ½ teaspoon garlic powder
- ⅓ cup finely diced onion
- Hard boiled eggs, chopped
- Chives optional

Directions

1. Cook the cauliflower either on the stove or microwave. Cool.
2. Whisk dressing: mayonnaise, apple cider vinegar, mustard and garlic powder.
3. Add onion and egg to cauliflower in a medium bowl.
4. Add dressing.
5. Add chives as a garnish and to add color to the salad.

Tips & Notes:

This is by far one of my favorite cauliflower recipes. I am still trying to embrace the cauliflower! I almost did not realize I was eating cauliflower and not potatoes; it is that good if you love potatoes. Really! And I love potatoes, but oxalates and potatoes do not play nicely together.

Broccoli Slaw

Serves 4

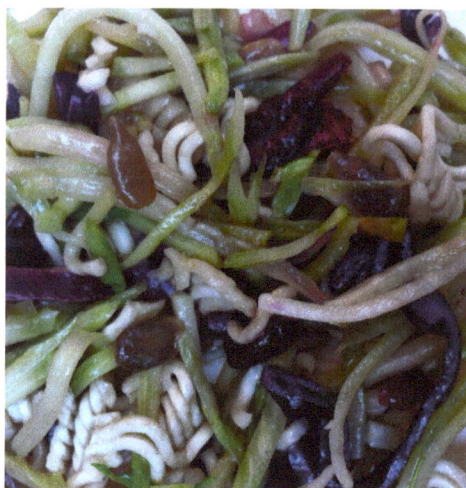

Ingredients

→ 1 bag broccoli slaw mix or grate your own without carrots (tutorial)
→ ¼ red Vidalia onion chopped or shredded

Dressing

→ ⅛ cup light mayonnaise
→ ½ tablespoon apple cider vinegar
→ ½ teaspoon sugar or sugar substitute
→ ½ lime juiced

Directions

1. Whisk together ingredients.
2. Add ½ of the dressing to the broccoli slaw.
3. Taste test the slaw with the dressing and check consistency.
4. Add more dressing if needed and serve remainder on the side.

Tips & Notes:

Carrots are frequently part of Broccoli Slaw. However, carrots are very high in oxalate; add shredded carrots for the oxalate friendly guests before you mix the slaw. Grate your own broccoli and cabbage slaw to make a healthy slaw.

Cold Spaghetti Salad
Serves 4

Ingredients

- Cooked spaghetti to serve 4
- 1 cup diced cucumbers
- 1 cup diced zucchini
- 1 cup diced squash
- 1 cup cauliflower or broccoli, break into small florets
- A few cherry tomatoes
- Light basil vinaigrette or Italian dressing

Directions

1. Cook four servings of spaghetti.
2. Remove from water and rinse with cold water.
3. Drain.
4. Place spaghetti in a serving dish and add vegetables.
5. Gently toss.
6. Add dressing to spaghetti and refrigerate one hour. This leaves time for the dressing to meld into the salad. If prepping the salad ahead of time keep spaghetti and vegetables separate until one hour before serving and then combine.

Tips & Notes:

Flexible is this salads' middle name. Choose your favorite vegetables. To keep this low oxalate keep the serving of spaghetti to one cup (12 mg oxalate) cooked and load up on the vegetables. Add mini mozzarella balls for the cheese fans.

SIDE DISHES

Crab Casserole

Serves 4

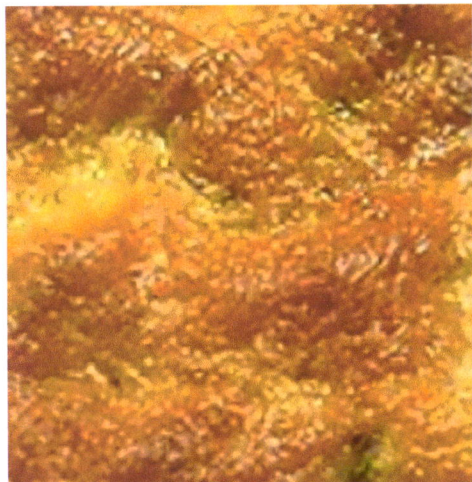

Ingredients

- → 1 six ounce can of crab meat, drained
- → 6 hard boiled eggs
- → 1 cup onion, chopped
- → 1 cup mayonnaise
- → 3/4 cup half and half
- → 1 cup bread crumbs
- → ½ crushed butter crackers for topping

Directions

1. Preheat oven to 350 degrees F.
2. Grease a 2 quart casserole dish with cooking spray.
3. Break up the crab meat into small chunks.
4. In a large bowl combine the crab meat, mayonnaise, eggs, onion, half and half, 1 cup bread crumbs.
5. Spread mixture into casserole dish.
6. Top with buttered crackers.
7. Bake 20–25 minutes until top is golden brown.

Tips & Notes:

Are you still thinking about the crab and egg combination? I was too and found I liked it! For obvious reasons the flavors of the egg and crab do dominate.

Riced Cauliflower Mash

Serves 4

Ingredients

- → 1 head cauliflower cut into florets
- → ½–1 stick butter
- → 6 ounces warmed milk
- → Salt to taste (wait until after made to taste test if salt is needed)

Directions

1. Steam the cauliflower until soft.
2. Remove from heat.
3. Add ½ stick butter into the bottom of a bowl.
4. Add the cauliflower to the ricer and rice into the bowl.
5. Mix the butter and cauliflower together with a wooden spoon. Check the consistency. Taste test.
6. Add more butter if needed.
7. Warm ¾ of a glass of milk in the microwave.
8. Gradually add the milk to the cauliflower and mix in.
9. This is a matter of personal preference. The more milk added the creamier the mash will become.
10. Salt and pepper to taste.

Tips & Notes:

One of my favorite kitchen hacks is the ricer. If you want mashed cauliflower that closest resembles the consistency of mashed potatoes then a ricer is a must have tool in your kitchen box of tricks.

Creamed Kale

Serves 2

Ingredients

- 1 pound of kale. Remove center stalk.
- 2 tablespoons butter
- ½ cup onion chopped
- ½ cup cream or half and half or milk
- Pepper to taste
- Grated parmesan cheese optional

Directions

1. Blanche the kale in water (can use slightly salted water if desired.)
2. Remove kale and put into cold water to stop cooking. Drain.
3. Cut kale into ribbons.
4. In a large skillet over medium heat melt the butter.
5. Then add the kale and cream.
6. Now reduce the heat to low and cook for 5 minutes. The cream will begin to thicken.
7. Add salt and pepper to taste and if desired add a sprinkle of grated parmesan cheese.

Tips & Notes:

I know you are still mourning the loss of spinach … ! Try creamed kale as an alternative. Kale seems to have a love hate relationship with its' consumer; if you are a fan, try it creamed. The type of milk or cream will determine the consistency.

Zoodles

Serves 2

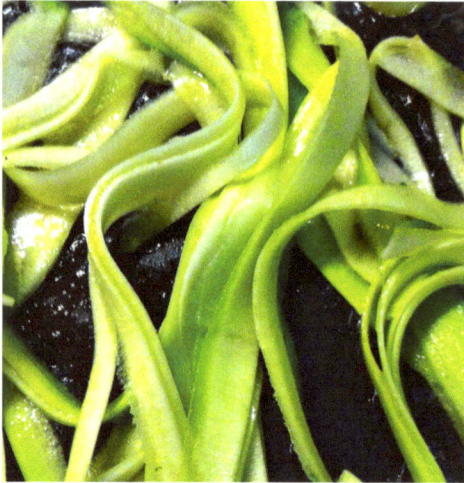

Ingredients

+ 2 medium zucchini
+ 2 tablespoons butter
+ 3 teaspoons minced garlic or 3 cloves
+ ¾ cup parmesan cheese
+ Cooking spray

Directions

1. Clean the zucchini.
2. Cut off the ends of both zucchini so the ends are flat.
3. On a cutting board stand one zucchini with the flat side down.
4. Take a potato peeler and using long vertical strokes thinly slice the zucchini.
5. Repeat for second zucchini.
6. Spray a large skillet with cooking spray. Heat the skillet on medium high heat.
7. Melt the butter and add the garlic.
8. Quickly saute the garlic. Garlic cooks very quickly.
9. Add the zoodles and cook for approximately 3–5 minutes. Careful! Overcooking will lead to mushy zoodles; aim for el dente.
10. Remove from pan and toss with parmesan cheese.

Tips & Notes:

Jazz up the zoodles with Italian seasoning if desired or low oxalate herbs such as chives. A dash of sea salt can be added; oxalate friendly can add pepper.

Grilled Watermelon

Serves many

Ingredients

- → Watermelon sliced into thick quarter. Leave on rind.
- → Olive Oil
- → Sea salt

Directions

1. Preheat your electric grill to medium high heat or fire up the coals.
2. Coat each slice of watermelon on both sides with olive oil.
3. Add a dash of sea salt to each side of watermelon.
4. Grill about one minute per side. Flip when grill marks develop.
5. Serve.

Tips & Notes:

Who knew you could grill a watermelon? The watermelon needs to be thickly sliced so the watermelon can be flipped with tongs. Lime zest is a nice addition to kick up the flavor.

Vegetable & Cheese Rice Bake

Serves 4

Ingredients

→ ½ bag frozen broccoli thawed
→ ½ bag frozen cauliflower thawed
→ 1 cup cooked rice
→ 4 ounces shredded sharp cheddar cheese
→ ½ small onion chopped
→ 1 can of cream of chicken soup
→ 1 tablespoon butter

Directions

1. Preheat oven to 350 degrees F.
2. In a small pan melt the butter and saute the onion.
3. In a large bowl mix all ingredients together.
4. Bake in a 2 quart baking dish for 45 minutes to 1 hour.

Tips & Notes:

This is the classic homemade casserole. Use low salt cheese, low salt soup or gluten free soup if desired. Sharp cheese works the best for this casserole. Add diced chicken and make a meal.

APPETIZERS/ SNACKS

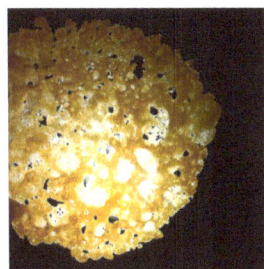

Mini Cherry Tomato BLT

Serves many

Ingredients

→ 28 cherry tomatoes
→ 7 bacon strips, crispy and crumbled
→ ½ cup mayonnaise
→ ⅓ cup chopped green onions
→ 3 tablespoons grated Parmesan cheese
→ 2 tablespoons minced fresh parsley optional

Directions

1. Cut the tops off of each tomato. Just slice off the very top of the cherry tomato.
2. Scoop out the inside of each tomato. Discard the pulp.
3. Turn the tomatoes upside down on a sheet of paper towel.
4. Let the tomatoes drain on the paper towel.
5. Mix the filling in a small bowl. combine the crumbled bacon, mayonnaise, onions, cheese, and parsley.
6. Spoon the mixing into each tomato.
7. Let the tomatoes chill for a minimum of 2 hours in the refrigerator.
8. Arrange the tomatoes in a platter and sprinkle tops with crumbled bacon.

Tips & Notes:

Low fat mayonnaise works very well in this recipe as does turkey bacon! For your oxalate friendly guests add 2 tablespoons celery.

Cucumber Rounds

Serves many

Ingredients

- → 1 seedless cucumber
- → Cream Cheese in a tub
- → Fresh herbs (I use chives)

Directions

1. Soften the cream cheese to room temperature.
2. Slice the ends off the cucumber.
3. Cut the cucumber into slices measuring ½ inch per slice.
4. Gently scoop out the middle of each slice until a thin layer of cucumber remains at the bottom of the newly created hole. (I use a ½ teaspoon.)
5. Lay out paper towel.
6. Flip over each cucumber to drain the water. The cream cheese adheres better to the cucumber with less water. I actually leave the cucumber slices to drain for at least an hour.
7. Fill a disposable decorating bag with the cream cheese. (Or use a quart size plastic bag and snip the end.)
8. Mix the softened cream cheese with fresh low oxalate herbs or use the already flavored cream cheese in a tub.
9. Pipe the cream cheese into the middle of each cucumber slice.
10. If desired top the Cucumber Round with chives or a low oxalate herb of your choice.

Tips & Notes:

Purchase cream cheese in a tub flavored with your favorite herbs. Use low fat or fat free cream cheese to lower the fat content.

Zucchini Crisps

Serves many

Ingredients

- → 2 medium size zucchinis, sliced thin
- → 2 tablespoons olive oil oven
- → 1 egg beaten
- → ½ cup bread crumbs (can use gluten free)
- → ½ cup grated parmesan cheese
- → Cooking spray if using air fryer

Directions

1. Slice the zucchini thin.
2. Remove excess moisture from zucchini slices by patting with a paper towel. The key for a crisp is to remove as much of the moisture as possible.
3. Prepare your assembly line: one bowl with olive oil, one bowl with breadcrumbs and parmesan cheese and one bowl with the beaten egg.
4. Oven: Line a 13" by 9" baking pan with parchment paper. Preheat oven to 350 degrees.
5. Dip each zucchini into olive oil, then egg, then breadcrumbs.
6. Place 1–2 inches apart on the baking pan.
7. Bake about 15–17 minutes until crispy.

Air Fryer:

1. Omit the olive oil and use cooking spray.
2. Instead of dipping each slice into olive oil, spray the zucchini with cooking spray.
3. Preheat air fryer to 350 degrees.
4. Place prepared crisps into air fryer in batches.
5. Air Fry for 8 minutes.

Tips & Notes:

Removing the water is the key to the crisp. Experiment with your air fryer or oven as the cooking time will slightly vary depending upon how much water was removed from the zucchini and the strength of your oven.

Parmesan Crisps

Serves many

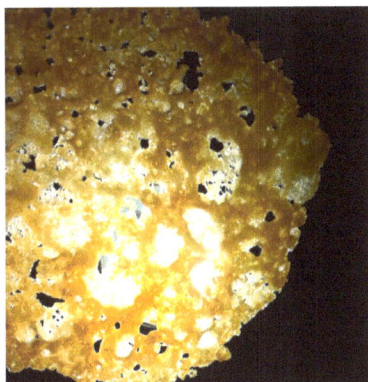

Ingredients

→ 1 tablespoon grated parmesan cheese
→ Optional: Add low oxalate herbs of your choice

Directions

Microwave Single Serve:

1. Place 1 tablespoons of parmesan cheese on a microwave safe plate. I mound the cheese.
2. The cooking time is dependent upon the strength of your microwave.
3. Microwave on high for 30 seconds. Plan on 20–30 seconds per crisp.
4. A little trial and error is involved depending upon the type of parmesan cheese, the strength of the microwave and how crispy you prefer your crisp.

Oven Batch:

1. Use a 13" by 9" baking pan.
2. Line the pan with parchment paper.
3. Mound 1 tablespoons of parmesan cheese per crisp. The amount of parmesan cheese determines the width of the crisp.
4. Space the mounds 1–2 inches apart on the parchment paper.
5. Bake at 400 degrees for 3.5 minutes.
6. Store in an air tight container.

Tips & Notes:

Parmesan crisps are an easy and quick snack or add to your favorite salad or soup! There are brands of low fat ready made parmesan cheese; but be cognizant of the sodium value. One crisp is a very nice size to add to low oxalate salad for crunch; a handful of crisps is for the cheese loving friend with no salt or oxalate issues.

Holiday Vegetable Tree – DIY

Serves many

Ingredients

- → Fresh broccoli
- → Fresh cauliflower
- → Red grape tomatoes
- → Red onion
- → Yellow squash
- → Assorted peppers
- → Favorite firm yellow cheese
- → Firm mozzarella cheese cut into a thick square
- → metal cookie cutters
- → 12″ foam cone, disposable plate, aluminum foil, toothpicks
- → glue gun

Directions

1. Begin with creating your tree base by wrapping a foam cone (size is your choice) with foil.
2. Attach cone to a disposable serving plate with the glue gun.
3. Prepare your vegetables and toothpicks.
4. Break apart the broccoli and cauliflower florets, cut the squash and onions into medium size shapes (think one bite size.)
5. Use an assembly line to insert toothpicks into the vegetables. Assembly line style will make the process move quicker.
6. Decide ahead of time if you would like a pattern to your vegetable tree design or a random pattern of vegetables on the tree.
7. Begin assembling the tree. This does take patience. Broccoli and cauliflower are heavy so the tree may need to be propped until completion.
8. Arrange your vegetables on the tree.
9. Once the tree is fully loaded with vegetables the tree will stand straight on the plate.
10. The Christmas version: Use the broccoli as tree, tomatoes as the garland and cheese as the ornaments.
11. For ornaments, use a metal cookie cutter to cut 'cheese cookies' and add to the tree with toothpicks.

Tips & Notes:

Why is there a glue gun in my ingredient list you ask? This is a DIY Vegetable Centerpiece that will satisfy all your guests and very oxalate friendly. Serve this as your appetizer and guests will surround the tree and can choose their favorite veggie. Add dipping sauce to enjoy with your tree!

Grandma's Crustades

Serves many

Ingredients

→ 1 loaf bread or gluten free bread or oat bread

→ Softened butter

→ Favorite low oxalate salad (chicken, tuna, crab all work well)

Directions

1. Preheat oven to 325 degrees.
2. Layout bread on a cutting board and cut off the crusts.
3. With a rolling pin roll each slice into a nice flat slice of bread.
4. Using a 2.5 inch circle cookie cutter, cut a 2.5" round from each piece of bread.
5. Butter each slice on both sides.
6. In a mini muffin pan ease each slice into a muffin cup. A wavy edge will be created around each bread cup.
7. Bake 10–15 minutes. I begin checking at the 10 minute mark. Remove when the outside of the bread cup is golden brown.
8. Cool.
9. Fill crustades with your favorite low oxalate salad and serve!
10. Recipe makes the number of bread slices in a loaf which is usually 20–24 crustades.

Tips & Notes:

Crustades can be made with any type of bread that is dense or medium firm. Very soft bread is not recommended for Grandma's Crustades. The bread scraps make wonderful homemade croutons or bread crumbs!

Squash Salsa

Serves many

Ingredients

→ 2 tablespoons oil
→ 1 cup zucchini diced
→ 1 cup yellow squash diced
→ 1 cup cantaloupe diced
→ ½ cup green pepper * diced
→ Optional: Dash of sea salt

Directions

1. Using a large skillet heat oil over medium to high heat. Add the zucchini, pepper and squash to saute until tender (about 2 minutes.)
2. Remove from heat and drain on paper towels.
3. Immediately refrigerate for one hour.
4. Add cantaloupe and serve!

Tips & Notes:

*½ cup of green pepper has 5 mg of oxalate. To bump up the flavor for the oxalate friendly add pepper or red/yellow diced peppers.

Pretzel and Cream Cheese Snacks

Serves many

Ingredients

→ Pretzels Sticks—low salt, no salt, gluten free
→ Cream Cheese

Directions

1. Simply dip your pretzel into the cream cheese and enjoy!
2. Of course moderation is the key and monitor the serving size of the cream cheese per pretzel… I admit that as a cream cheese fan I could probably just eat the cream cheese with a side of pretzels!

Tips & Notes:

Did you do a double take on this food combo? I did when my friend Jim first alerted me to this yummy snack; this combination never occurred to me! If you love the crunch of a pretzel and cream cheese then you will absolutely enjoy the two combined as a snack.

Salty and crunchy snacks are very difficult when following a low oxalate menu. Pretzels are one of the acceptable crunchy snacks measured at 5 mg oxalate per 1 ounce. But one ounce of pretzel sticks is a nice snack size combined with the calcium friendly cream cheese.

Holiday Puffcorn
Serves many

Ingredients
→ One bag of puffcorn
→ 1 cup of white chocolate or white chocolate chips
→ Holiday sprinkles optional

Directions
1. Line a 13" by 9" baking pan with parchment paper. One bag will take 2 baking sheets.
2. Lay the puffcorn in a single layer.
3. Melt the white chocolate in the microwave.
4. Drizzle melted chocolate over the puffcorn.
5. Add holiday sprinkles if desired.
6. Put the pan(s) into the refrigerator for 10 minutes to set the puffcorn.
7. Remove puffcorn from refrigerator and break apart into snack sizes.
8. Store in an air tight container.

Tips & Notes:

Sweet and salty alert! I am keeping it real and without apologies forewarn this is a treat. A treat which is always a crowd pleaser for your guests (the bowl will disappear like magic), but does contain a dose of sugar and salt. This is a make your choice recipe for an oxalate menu—where do you want to allocate your oxalates? For those with a sweet tooth this is a special treat and while your guests may very well eat handfuls; oxalate watchers enjoy a few…

Puffcorn is the cousin of popcorn; popcorn without hulls. Look for puffcorn in the snack section of your local market.

Apple Banana Sushi

Serves many

Ingredients

- → Banana
- → Gluten-Free Apple Butter
- → Gluten-Free Krispy Cereal (brand of your choice)

Directions

1. Peel the banana.
2. Spread apple butter on the outside of banana.
3. Spread the cereal on a paper plate.
4. Roll banana in the cereal mixture.
5. Cut the finished sushi into bite size slices.

Tips & Notes:

This is an easy and healthy snack or even part of breakfast! Bring the napkins though as it can be a tad messy; yummy but a little messy to eat. Substitute the apple butter with sun butter for the I miss peanut butter fans and moderate the serving size.

Rice Cakes With Fruit & Yogurt

Serves many

Ingredients

→ Favorite brand of rice cakes
→ Favorite brand of plain or vanilla yogurt
→ Fresh low oxalate fruit—banana
→ Optional: Dash of honey

Directions

1. Great snack anytime of the day! Use with or without low oxalate fruits.
2. Spread yogurt on a rice cake and spread with yogurt.
3. Add toppings of your choice: fruit or a dash of honey or both!

Tips & Notes:

Double the fun by making a rice cake sandwich!

Reduce the sodium and fat content with fat free and low sodium rice cakes.

Flaxseed Chips

Serves many

Ingredients

- → ½ cup flaxseed meal
- → ⅛ cup water
- → 1 pinch salt

Directions

1. Preheat your oven to 350 degrees.
2. Preheat your medium size skillet to medium high heat. You will be creating the flaxseed dough in the heated skillet.
3. Add the flaxseed meal, water and salt to the skillet.
4. Work the ingredients around the skillet with a spatula. As the dough begins to combine work the ingredients into a ball in the middle of the skillet.
5. Remove the ball from the skillet.
6. Using the sandwich method to roll out the dough. Place the ball between two pieces of parchment paper or wax paper. I prefer parchment paper.
7. Roll the dough as thin as possible between the sheets of paper.
8. Using a sharp knife or pizza cutter, cut the dough into bite size chips. The size is your preference.
9. Transfer the chips to a parchment lined baking sheet.
10. Bake the chips for 8 to 12 minutes. I begin checking the chips for crispness at 8 minutes.
11. For mini chips I bake for 6 minutes.
12. Remove when chips are crisp.

Tips & Notes:

Flaxseed Chips are a great alternative for those who miss nuts. The chips have a nice nutty flavor and are perfect for dipping, salsa or a healthy snack. You can make your own flaxseed meal from flax seeds too!

DESSERTS

Blueberry Pops
Makes Four

Ingredients

- 1 pint of fresh blueberries
- ¼ cup honey
- ¼ cup water

Directions

1. Combine ingredients in a blender.
2. Blend until smooth.
3. Pour into popsicle molds.
4. Freeze a minimum of 4 hours.

Tips & Notes:

Use your favorite fruit to make these all natural fruit pops. Watermelon and black cherries work great too!

Hello Dolly Bars

Makes 24 bars

Ingredients

- → 1 ½ cups corn flake crumbs
- → ½ cup unsalted butter
- → 1 cup white chocolate chips
- → 1 cup butterscotch chips
- → 1 cup sunflower seeds
- → 1 ⅓ cups shredded coconut
- → 1 14 oz. can sweetened condensed milk

Directions

1. Heat oven to 350 degrees F.
2. Line a 13" X 9" baking pan with parchment paper.
3. Cut up butter, place in baking pan and place in oven until butter is melted.
4. Add cornflake crumbs to butter and lightly mix.
5. Lightly press the mixture into a cornflake crumb layer.
6. Sprinkle sunflower nuts over the cornflake crumb layer.
7. Sprinkle white chocolate chips over the cornflake crumb layer.
8. Sprinkle butterscotch chips over the cornflake crumb layer.
9. Pour condensed milk over mixture.
10. Sprinkle coconut over top of bars.
11. Cook at 350 degrees for 25 minutes. The coconut should be very lightly browned.
12. Cool. Using the parchment paper as handles lift the Low Oxalate Hello Dolly Bars out of the baking pan.
13. Cut into squares.

Tips & Notes:

This is a dessert and it makes no apologies for its' sugar content. One little square absolutely will satisfy the sweet tooth while the family eats the remainder. Sunflower seeds are high at 12 mg per cup, but that is one cup sprinkled throughout an entire pan of bars. Nonetheless while this is a low oxalate version; both versions are high in sugar.

Mom's Banana Pudding

Serves 4–6

Ingredients

→ 12 vanilla wafers or make your own (see next recipe)
→ 2 medium bananas sliced
→ 8 ounces cream cheese softened
→ ¼ cup sugar
→ ½ teaspoon vanilla
→ 1 cup whipping cream

Directions

1. Line bottom and sides of a 1 quart bowl with wafers.
2. Combine softened cream cheese, sugar, vanilla and mix until well blended.
3. Fold in bananas.
4. Spoon mixture over the wafers.
5. Chill.

Tips & Notes:

Another recipe from the family vault; old school pudding. If you like pudding many are actually oxalate friendly! Vanilla and banana pudding are great choices. Check out the vanilla wafer recipe to make your own with coconut flour.

Coconut Flour Nilla Wafers–Sugar Free

Makes approximately 18–20 cookies

Ingredients

- ½ cup coconut flour
- ½ cup Swerve or sugar substitute
- ½ teaspoon salt
- ½ teaspoon baking powder
- ½ cup butter unsalted
- 2 teaspoons vanilla extract
- 2 egg yolks
- ½ teaspoon vanilla liquid stevia

Directions

1. Add flour, sugar, salt, baking powder to a large bowl and blend.
2. Add butter, egg yolks, extract and blend.
3. Lay out a sheet of parchment paper or wax paper.
4. Add the wafer dough and form a long roll (the cookies will be sliced later.)
5. Wrap the cookie log and refrigerate 30 minutes.
6. Line a baking sheet with parchment paper.
7. Remove cookie log from refrigerator and slice into cookies.
8. Bake 12–13 minutes, depending upon your oven. Check at 12 minutes.
9. Remove cookies from oven when edges begin to brown.
10. Let cookies sit on a baking rack for 10 minutes.
11. Store in an air tight container.

Tips & Notes:

The temperature of the oven, desired width of cookie and type of coconut flour used will vary the baking time. Thinner cookies equal less baking time.

Watermelon Ice

Makes one 8" pan

Ingredients

→ 2 cups seedless watermelon
→ 2 tablespoons honey or agave
→ 1 tablespoon lemon juice
→ 1 ½ cups of ice cubes

Directions

1. Combine ingredients in a blender.
2. Blend on high until smooth.
3. Pour mixture into an 8" baking dish or bowl.
4. Freeze until the mixture is slushy about 30–45 minutes.
5. Remove from freezer.
6. Scrape with a fork.
7. Put back into freezer for a minimum of 2 hours. (I put it in overnight.)
8. Serve with mint or basil leaves.

Tips & Notes:

Watermelon is one of the best ways to add water to your menu without the oxalates. Love this watermelon ice which adds a different twist to watermelon. If you need to sweeten, add a dash of sugar or sugar substitute.

So easy! So fun! So festive! Watermelon ice cubes are a great way to incorporate watermelon into your menu and perfect for hotter weather.

Meringue Puffs
Makes 20–24 puffs

Ingredients
→ 2 egg whites (room temperature)
→ ¼ teaspoon cream of tartar
→ ½ cup sugar
→ ½ teaspoon vanilla extract (optional)

Directions
1. Line a baking sheet with parchment paper. Preheat oven to 225 degrees F.
2. Beat egg whites in a medium size bowl until light and foamy.
3. Add cream of tartar and beat until peaks form.
4. Slowly add a bit of sugar, beat until dissolved and repeat.
5. Add the mixture to a pastry bag (or use a baggie and cut off the end!) to pipe the puffs onto the baking sheet.
6. Space the puffs about 2 inches apart.
7. Remember! What you see is what you will get; these puffs do not spread.
8. Bake for 45 minutes. Stop and step away from the oven for one hour. Let the puffs set and cool.
9. Store in air tight containers.

Tips & Notes:
The key to a meringue puff is allowing enough time for the cooked puff to set in the oven after baking. The goal is a puff which is light on the inside and crunchy on the outside. I also like to make the puffs with meringue powder as an egg white substitute.

Chocolate Covered Rice Cake

Serves many

Ingredients

→ Rice cake, brand of your preference. Can use low salt or fat free rice cakes.
→ Melted white chocolate

Directions

1. Line a baking pan with parchment paper.
2. Melt the chocolate in the microwave. I begin with melting the chocolate at 30 seconds on high then in 15 second increments. The melting time does differ depending upon the chocolate and strength of microwave.
3. Using tongs dip the rice cake into the chocolate and swirl around the bowl for an even covering.
4. Lay the rice cake on the parchment paper.
5. Add sprinkles if desired.
6. Put the rice cakes into the refrigerator to set the chocolate.
7. Store in air tight containers.

Tips & Notes:

After I discovered how much I like rice cakes (surprise!) I decided to dress up the rice cake with white chocolate and dark chocolate (for the oxalate friendly). Yummy! This is a great recipe to batch make and use whichever type of chocolate your family and friends prefer. Again, this is a treat for oxalate watchers and white chocolate is preferred.

Maple Fudge

Serves many

Ingredients

- ½ cup maple syrup
- ⅓ cup smooth sun butter
- ¼ cup coconut oil
- 1 teaspoons vanilla extract

Directions

1. Line 8" by 8" glass pan with parchment or wax paper.
2. Combine sun butter, syrup and coconut oil into a small saucepan.
3. Over medium heat stir constantly (just like making pudding) until mixture is a smooth consistency.
4. Bring the mixture to a boil.
5. Boil for approximately 2 minutes until mixture thickens (again like pudding).
6. Stir in the vanilla extract.
7. Pour into prepared pan.
8. Place in freezer until the fudge is firmly set.
9. Very easy to remove fudge from the pan with the parchment paper lining.
10. Cut fudge into pieces.

Tips & Notes:

This is sweet! Very sweet and a little square will go along way. One little square is a treat for oxalate watchers, but has the advantage of not using chocolate. Not recommended if sugar content is a concern. Sun butter is an alternative to peanut butter and the amount is small when spread throughout an entire recipe.

Butterscotch Pudding or Pie

Ingredients

- → 1 ½ cups light brown sugar
- → ¼ cup cornstarch
- → ¼ teaspoon salt
- → 3 cups milk, whole = creamier
- → 4 egg yolks
- → 2 tablespoons unsalted butter

Directions

1. In a medium sauce pan combine the sugar, salt and cornstarch.
2. In a bowl combine and whisk the egg yolks and milk.
3. Add the egg/milk mixture to the pan.
4. On medium heat stir the mixture until bubbly. Be patient as this is homemade pudding! Plan on standing and stirring for 10–12 minutes.
5. Now add the butter and stir.
6. Pudding is now ready to serve warm or can be served cold later.
7. Add a dollop of whipped cream or ….
8. Make a butterscotch pudding pie by pouring pudding into a prepared graham cracker crust pie shell (or make your own pie crust from graham crackers.)

Tips & Notes:

Butterscotch pudding has a healthy dose of calcium—yeah! Moderation remains the key with desserts and low oxalates. Those with sweet tooths face difficult obstacles finding low oxalate desserts—enjoy one serving!

Stop in and visit for more low oxalate information at:

The Savvy Age
https://thesavvyage.com/

THE SAVVY AGE
food. family. diy.

Facebook Page
https://www.facebook.com/lowoxcookbook/

Low
Oxalate
Recipes

Facebook Closed Group
Request access at: https://www.facebook.com/groups/247318615721012/

Low Oxalate
FOODIES

creative. lox. recipes.

Resources

The definition for low oxalate of the recipes in this book is the Harvard list. Searching the internet does provide a variety of information which can be conflicting and not authoritative. Please vet the source carefully. The following are sources of information I have found helpful.

Harvard Master List 2007

https://regepi.bwh.harvard.edu/health/Oxalate/files

I consider this the gold standard of measuring low oxalate values of foods. Easy to use comprehensive and extensive spreadsheet of oxalate values of foods. However, notice the date. Due to further research, the master list needed some updating ... enter the University Of Chicago

University Of Chicago

http://kidneystones.uchicago.edu/

Definitely one of my favorite sites. Concentrates on kidney stone prevention and the role of diet in forming kidney stones of all varieties.

The team at University headed by Dr. Fred Coe and Jill Harris keep an updated site and working in tandem with associated experts have updated the Harvard master list for the top 180 high oxalate foods.

The list is user friendly and the team takes a proactive moderate approach to modifying your diet to a low oxalate diet if needed. Questions are encouraged and answered on the site. This is a proactive patient approach website.

University Of Maryland

http://ummidtown.org/health/medical/reports/articles/kidney-stones

In depth Patient Education Report which includes the causes, diagnosis techniques, prevention and dietary suggestions dependent on type of kidney stone.

University Of Michigan Nephrology Stone Clinic

http://www.med.umich.edu/intmed/nephrology/PATIENTS/stone.htm

Comprehensive site for kidney stones, kidney diets and kidney issues. Young Adult and geriatric kidney disease clinics.

University of Pittsburgh Low Oxalate Diet

http://www.upmc.com/patients-visitors/education/nutrition/Pages/low-oxalate-diet.aspx

Quick to read charts of low and high oxalate foods.

National Institute Of Diabetes and Digestive and Kidney Diseases

http://www.niddk.nih.gov/health-information/health-topics/urologic-disease/kidney-stones-in-adults/Pages/facts.aspx

In depth site which contains information for all types of kidney disorders. Explanation of the role of diet and low oxalates. Clinical trial information for those interested.

Cleveland Clinic Oxalate Controlled Diet

http://my.clevelandclinic.org/services/urology-kidney/treatments-procedures/kidney-stones-oxalate-controlled-diet

Top six suggestions for oxalate control to decrease the risk of kidney stone formation.

Websites:

Kidney Stoners

Kidneystoners.org

A one stop shop for the layman with information which will answer your questions. Every question. Bookmark this site although the activity on the site does vary.

Yahoo Group Trying Low Oxalates

Search Yahoo Groups for Trying Low Oxalates aka TLO. Founded in 2005 by Susan Owens. This is a closed group so one must apply for entry. Very active listserv group; great site to search for oxalate content of foods not found on the major lists. Interested listmates all share an interest in low oxalate foods for a variety of reasons.

Be sure to investigate the >Files option which has a multitude of tips, tricks and oxalate resources whether you are researching, cooking or considering a low oxalate food or diet.

Low Oxalate Info

http://lowoxalateinfo.com/

Low oxalate recipes plus the trials and errors of low oxalate ingredient substitution. Site has not been active since 2014, but does contain recent (within past five years) low oxalate food information and values.

www.ingramcontent.com/pod-product-compliance
Lightning Source LLC
Chambersburg PA
CBHW041431090426
42744CB00003B/31